Journey Through History

The Renaissance

Translation: Jean Grasso Fitzpatrick

English translation © Copyright 1988 by Barron's Educational Series, Inc.

© Parramón Ediciones, S.A.
First Edition, February 1988
The title of the Spanish edition is *El renacimiento*

All inquiries should be addressed to:
Barron's Educational Series, Inc.
250 Wireless Boulevard
Hauppauge, New York 11788

Library of Congress Catalog Card No. 88-10386
International Standard Book No. 0-8120-3396-5
Library of Congress Cataloging-in-Publication Data

Vergés, Gloria.
  [Renacimiento. English]
  The Renaissance / [illustrated by] Carme Peris ; [written by]
Gloria & Oriol Vergés ; [translation, Jean Grasso Fitzpatrick]. —
1st ed.
    p. cm. — (Journey through history)
  Translation of: Renacimiento.
  Summary: An illustrated history of the Renaissance period, with a
fictional story involving children to depict the time in history.
  ISBN 0-8120-3396-5
  1. Renaissance—Juvenile literature.   [1. Renaissance.]
I. Peris, Carme, ill.   II. Vergés, Oriol.   III. Title.   IV. Series:
Vergés, Gloria. Viaje a través de la historia. English.
D228.V4413 1988
909.2'1—dc19   88-10386
                                                              CIP
                                                               AC

Printed in Spain by Sirven Grafic
Legal Deposit: B-39.933-88

90   98765432

Journey Through History

The Renaissance

Carme Peris
Glòria & Oriol Vergés

BARRON'S

New York • Toronto • Sydney

As the Middle Ages drew to a close, a great age of exploration and discovery began. This period has been named the *Renaissance*, from the French word meaning "rebirth."

During the Renaissance, the nobles and princes of Italy and other countries of Europe supported writers and poets. As a result, they could dedicate themselves to their work and not worry about making a living. These poets lived in palaces and took part in court festivals. They wrote poems of love or religion, not in Latin or Greek, as poets had in the past. Instead, they used Italian, French, Spanish, or German—the languages that were spoken on the streets and in town squares. Now everyone could understand poetry and enjoy it.

"Don't touch anything! Aren't the achievements of Leonardo da Vinci amazing?"

"My father says he's one of the most intelligent people who ever lived."

Flying a plane, or traveling underwater were only dreams in those days. But the people of the Renaissance were so fascinated by science that some of them designed machines to make these dreams come true. Most of these inventions did not work, however, because proper materials and adequate motors were not yet available. Today, people are still amazed at the abilities of "Renaissance men" who studied human anatomy and the flight of birds, and painted beautifully as well.

The invention of moveable type—letters that could be lined up in wooden cases, inked, and printed on sheets of paper—was a great step forward. Printing meant that books could be quickly and beautifully reproduced. They no longer had to be done by hand, and many copies could be made of each title. From then on, people could study works written in far-off countries and buy poetry books or stories in bookstores.

"Look at how readable this type is...and see how clearly the page is printed!"

"When I'm a merchant like my father, I'm going to buy lots of books for my library instead of having to read them at the convent library."

The popes lived in a part of Rome called the *Vatican*. They wanted St. Peter's Church and their palaces in the Vatican to be impressive and beautiful. This way, they reasoned, the faithful in Italy and the rest of the world would be amazed by their achievements. The Renaissance painters decorated the chapels and halls of the Vatican. They discovered new techniques and, with the help of their assistants, created huge paintings on the ceilings and walls of the palaces. These paintings, called *frescoes*, were of religious scenes and events from ancient Greek and Roman legends.

Many art historians believe that the perfection of the human figure, and the glowing colors of Renaissance painting have never been surpassed.

The recovery of sculptures from classical Greece and Rome suggested to Renaissance artists the idea of studying the human body and depicting its beauty. Sculptors worked with blocks of white or pink marble, most of it from quarries in Carrara, Italy. They also cast enormous bronze figures of soldiers on horseback and displayed them in city streets and plazas, to promote the pride of the citizens.

"Careful! Don't disturb Master Michelangelo. If we distract him, he will scold us."

Renaissance geographers were eager to learn whether the legends about monsters and giants living in the Atlantic Ocean were true. They were also curious to find out what lands lay across the sea.

There were those—like Christopher Columbus—who believed the earth was round, and that therefore they could reach the Indies by sailing west. This would make it possible for Europeans to transport precious goods—cinnamon, silks, jewels, and perfumes—without having to cross the lands controlled by the Moslems.

When Columbus landed in the islands of the Antilles, he believed that he was in a previously undiscovered part of the Far East. In reality, he had arrived on the doorstep of a new continent. It came to be called America, after Amerigo Vespucci, who was the first to realize Columbus's mistake.

In America, the natives had developed important civilizations that were very different from those of Greece, Rome, or the European Middle Ages. In their societies, warriors, priests, and kings ruled powerful empires. They lived in cities, worshipped their gods in great temples, and transported their goods along wide and well-built roads. When the Europeans colonized these lands, the meeting between the two cultures was very violent, because the new arrivals did not respect the customs of the Aztecs of Mexico, the Maya in the Yucatan, or the Incas of Peru.

"Poor sailors! They made the first trip around the world!"

"It was terrible, they say. They suffered through great storms and were so hungry that they even had to eat their leather belts."

"Even worse, when they went ashore to stock up on water, the Indians attacked them and killed Captain Magellan and many of his crew. Fortunately, Juan Sebastian made sure the expedition arrived at its destination!"

The first around-the-world trip was one of history's most dramatic adventures. Those brave sailors finally proved that the earth is round, and helped open new shipping routes.

"My father is very pleased. The trip was a success. His boat has returned full of precious cargo."

"Of course! Now he will sell his goods and use the money he earns to plan another voyage."

One result of the great voyages was that merchants became rich. As soon as a ship came in with a cargo of precious goods, they planned another voyage. Wealth grew quickly in the hands of the merchants. Sometimes they borrowed money from bankers who charged *interest*. That means that the bankers were repaid more money than they had originally lent. Thus, the voyages brought great wealth to people other than the merchants themselves.

People's curiosity during the Renaissance was not limited to discovering and exploring new seas and new lands. They also wanted to know the secrets of the stars and the laws that governed the motion of the planets. They proved that the sun is a star and that the earth revolves around it. They also discovered new planets. All this was achieved thanks to the invention of the telescope, which magnified our view of the heavens.

"We were awake all night looking at the stars!"
"Well, there are a lot more stars than the ones we can see through a telescope. It would be wonderful to be able to count them all!"

In the early days of printing, the Bible was one of the most widely published books. Martin Luther, a German monk, translated it and recommended that the faithful read it and try to understand it. Later, Luther left the Church of Rome because he did not agree with some of its basic principles and practices. Many Christians followed Luther and created the Reformed churches in Europe and, later, in America.

"It's not easy to understand the Bible."
"No, but my father and mother read a passage every day before dinner."

"That attack by Moslem pirates was terrible! Last year was the plague and bad harvest, and now the pirates are robbing us and destroying our houses."

"In a few years I'm going to go to the city and learn a trade. Life in the country is too hard."

Although living conditions improved in the cities, the peasants in the countryside continued to suffer endless misery. People in the cities felt freer. They were not dependent on a lord, noble, or bishop—unlike the peasants who could still be mistreated by their feudal lords.

During the Renaissance, the theater also underwent a great change. Religious pageants and shows were no longer put on only in churches or in the town squares, but in the first buildings especially made for actors to perform plays. The main characters of the tragedies were heroes whose downfall was caused by love, hate, or ambition. The comedies poked fun at the faults and weaknesses of everyday people.

"We've been lucky. Today we can see another tragedy by William Shakespeare."

"My parents don't like to bring me to the theater. They say I'm still too young, but I've already seen all of this season's shows!"

The adventures of the Spaniard, Don Quixote and his squire, Sancho Panza, also became popular as soon as they appeared in print. Readers enjoyed Miguel de Cervantes' work because it reflected a period of time, the age of knighthood, which was already over and which was not well known to them.

Don Quixote represents the kind of people who try to reach an impossible ideal, while Sancho, on the other hand, sees life very realistically. They're two personality types that have always existed and always will.

The idea of the Renaissance—rebirth—grew from the curiosity that intellectuals and artists of the fifteenth and sixteenth centuries felt for classical culture; they wanted to see its rebirth. The period's most outstanding characteristics were people's curiosity, spirit of initiative, and thirst for adventure.

Patrons of the Arts

The Medicis of Florence, princes and bankers, were model patrons of the arts. From Florence and Rome, where the popes were patrons, the custom of supporting artists extended to all the developed countries of Europe.

Painting and Sculpture

Painting and sculpture were the most spectacular examples of the discovery of new techniques and themes. It's certainly appropriate for children to learn about the lives of some of the great Renaissance figures, but it's even more interesting for them to learn the differences between the Middle Ages and the Renaissance.

Humanism

In the Middle Ages life and thought revolved around religion. The Renaissance was more humanistic: human beings—their achievements and their beauty—were indisputably the focus of literary and artistic activity. But rather than discourage people's curiosity about the world around them, this humanism actually fostered it.

The "Renaissance Man"

Leonardo da Vinci is probably one of the most intelligent and restless people who ever lived. He is the prototype of the "universal man," one who embraces all the arts and all the sciences. Not only was he an artist, but he studied botany and biology, and anticipated future discoveries.

Travel and Exploration

After the Renaissance, Europeans ruled the world. From the discovery of America—thanks to Columbus's good luck and the spirit of adventure of the age—political and economic ambitions brought Europe far beyond its own shores.

The Conquistadors
Relations between Europeans and American cultures were very violent. This was due to the Spanish conquistadors' economic ambitions and to their cultural superiority complex which led them, on many occasions, to destroy the native cultures.

Religion
Although Luther's Reform was born of a personal experience, it reflected opinions common to many followers of the Roman church. In fact, the demand for interpretation of the Bible by ordinary people is one more demonstration of the individualism of Renaissance thought.

Literature
Two great writers, Cervantes and Shakespeare, created universal characters that reflect the passions, concerns, worries and desires common to people in all different ages and circumstances. Without doubt, they were both geniuses at portraying human vices and virtues.